LIVING AT BAGGAGE CLAIM

LIVING AT BAGGAGE CLAIM

Poems and other stories by

PAGES Matam

Button Publishing Inc.
Minneapolis
2026

LIVING AT BAGGAGE CLAIM
POETRY
AUTHOR: PAGES Matam
COVER DESIGN: Coral Black
AUTHOR PHOTO: Jamal Josef
EDITED BY: Imani Cezanne

◇

◇

Published by Button Poetry
Minneapolis, MN 55418 | http://www.buttonpoetry.com

◇

Manufactured in the United States of America
PRINT ISBN: 978-1-63834-154-3
EBOOK ISBN: 978-1-63834-158-1

First printing

Dedicated to everyone I've called home.

CONTENTS

Pack Light

A Brief Timeline of Sorrow

Many Tiny Revolutions

FOREWORD

Before you proceed to baggage claim, I'm gonna need you to grab some drinking water. Hydration is paramount for the journey ahead of you. For when these poems insist on being read aloud. On showing you what it means to be "water born." Filled with the only element capable of drowning you or carrying you to all the wheres & whos you call home.

PAGES Matam's second full-length collection arrives with a gracious but urgent invitation. The emotional weight you've been packing since before you were born? It's time to watch it spread across the conveyor belt. It's time to decide what you're willing to continue pulling forward.

Here, you may see an oversized bag holding a "father's throne of want," "a tongue without a mother," & "the ocean of your own undoing." Perhaps a duffel bag with "the bones of Go-Go" & "Ogun's first meal" lifted onto the shoulder of another "border-/less spirit, yearning to/belong somewhere."

Living At Baggage Claim moves as immigrants must—between languages, nations, histories, & ways of being (mis)understood. One poem may roll you into an intimate conversation, the next a prayer, punchline, science lesson, scene, spell, call to action. One verse may unzip a traditional poetic form or build a new hard-shell from scratch.

How fortunate are we that this Camerounian polymath's complex relationship with travel informs their refusal to allow language or genre to become another checkpoint. For us who are "shackled to the wind," PAGES crafts multiple routes to enter a singular text. PAGES flips dictionaries, federal forms, & screenplays into shelter for poetry's layovers. To proceed is to experience the abundance borderlessness makes possible.

Years before we met, "Unforgettable," the group slam piece PAGES wrote with Elizabeth Acevedo & G. Yamazawa, was a staple in my teaching artist curriculum. Even through a screen, that electrifying collaboration never failed to inspire my students to unpack & celebrate each other's origin stories.

When our paths eventually crossed during a virtual screenwriting workshop at the height of the COVID-19 pandemic, I came to understand this film-poet as a real-life Power Ranger—reaching beyond the page to cultivate a collective portal through which we can all visit our most liberated selves.

You can, but why read this vulnerable offering alone? What do you owe your inner child? When does the body stop being evidence of empire & transform into a site for healing? Joy? Unabashed pleasure? This agent of imagination has gifted us a multidisciplinary investigation bound to "unlock many soft songs" within you. Claim what's yours. Leave the rest circling on the carousel.

NOVA CYPRESS BLACK

"Look to yourself. You free.
Nothing and nobody is obliged to save you but you.
Seek your own land."

from "Home" by Toni Morrison

LIVING AT BAGGAGE CLAIM

Part 1 of a triptych

PACK LIGHT

I. CHANGED CHILD LEARNING OF HOME

Application For Immigrant Authorization

Department of Homeland Security
U.S. Citizenship and Immigration Services

1.Andi na sebã, *l'anglais linga na titi*

2.Uu lam na mwende anglais n'à muna di pa bol

3.L'anglais n'est que ma quatrième langue

▶ **START HERE - Type or print in black ink.**

Part 1. Reason for Applying

I am applying for (select **only one** box):

1.a. English is only my fourth language

1.b. the baby of the family, the one
my mouth spoils, favorite
by default, who may one day be sold
off by its siblings
in hopes to never return

1.c. all of my other tongues have grown jealous

Part 2. Information About You

Your Full Legal Name

in Cameroun we have over 200 dialects
that's over 200 ways
to say love,
to say family
to say I belong to something
that does not want to kill
me, that does not want to siphon the
gold from my flesh or the stories from my bones

Other Names Used

Provide all other names you have ever used, including aliases, maiden name, and nicknames. If you need extra space to complete this section, use the space provided in **Part 6. Additional Information**.

*changed child

*go back where you came from

*stifled promise

*boy

Zodiac : Tropical

☉	Sun	♋	Cancer	20°22'
☽	Moon	♋	Cancer	4°24'
☿	Mercury	♋	Cancer	0°20'
♀	Venus	♊	Gemini	15°05'

MY BIRTH CHART AS A CLEAVE OR

After nearly eleven months, my mother survived
–willed me a Cancer, though
his mistress, saw me still-born
to my father's throne of want. Dead
in this water, thicker than blood made bad
my mother, the stubborn Virgo,
unforgiving as the decision to stay in
his hurt. Mama learned where there's smoke, there's a
poison refusing the responsibility of hearts;
Mama says I was her only painless
birth, after my father's legs ran
like the making of a flame
trying not to become another burned home.

Placidus

I ASC ♏ Scorpio 11°01'

HOW I WAS BORN ALMOST TWO MONTHS LATE AFTER MY MOTHER WAS POISONED BY THE MISTRESS

& I was born a metaphor right time on the wrong day
conceived for Gemini but
I became a wave when I wasn't made heir,
beat of his heart, his kingdom of fire ignites
water can crack a rolling stone and
my father, the Leo, makes craters of women -
in his heart or his fist, fluent in
liar, can't see the truth he was the
crafting of a defiant miracle.
gift of stars re-aligning, a complication turned
out of my life, & I became
rainbow child, delivered kicking & screaming
because I refused to drown in all of their salt.

IT'S MORPHIN' TIME!

My accent is a Saturday morning cartoon.

Riddling others with laughter.

I am not meant to be a body.

Just a figment.

WAR-TORN

after Safia Elhillo

i grew up without a country
orphan flag, stubborn tongue

red dirt. a border-
less spirit, yearning to

belong somewhere

i grew up without a mother
orphaned fag, switchblade tongue

black hole. still heart
less child, working towards belonging

to myself.

i am a tongue without a mother,
or, i am a country filled with

longing to be the child
i never got to love before

i became a War.

PLEASE DON'T LET [THE BOY] BE MISUNDERSTOOD

I used to believe I looked like God.
I used to believe I was God,

a Black Moor,
Moor from the French root word *mort* meaning *death*
hence: I am Black death best served Kentucky fried.

I am Sierra Leone behind the glass
until every kiss begins with slave

I am triangular
trinity of trade and offense
hang time...
confused pitbull staring at Michael Vick on a cross

Say *he got that DAWG IN HIM,*
I guess it makes sense to hang us from things made of bark
to make your money grow from trees
the boy wants to grow up to become Apple pie
wants to fit in
square peg in American star

grow paper-chased teeth
model minority eyes blue
as the oceans that carried wood-wombs
or watched over your 19-hour coffin with metal wings
or as the history of a bruise turning into
a purple mountain majesty; you'll learn the strangeness of
this fruit of a million loom
-ing suns, cotton gin jaw
smile like you know irony is a cruel deity.

But vengeance is mine,
said the ~~Lord~~ boy.

THE BOY'S GENEALOGY OF GRIEF

it starts with the blade
– like every family does – the jagged
want to survive the choking vine

I come from a long line
of aches who often made *I love you*
sound like a splinter in their throats

everyone says I have her eyes,
but I do not share her gift of sight
she says: *you look just like your root*

with that same swagger of fated fruit,
blistered by longing. I know she still
loves him…even if she won't admit

that she wants to be in his mouth
as prey or as lover -
more than she hates being alone

staying where you're not wanted
is how you learn to never fall
far from the heartbreak.

BI'S POETICA

I shaped my first poem in the 7th grade inspired by an episode of Power Rangers after the yellow one I had a crush on saved a poet from the monster-of-the-week. He professes his warm airs thick with simile and what struck me most in that moment was the intense feeling of wanting someone like her to save me & someone like him to rhyme me into a love-soaked universe. In the 9th grade, the class clowns & cool kids watched the monster-of-my-every-week put me in a rear-naked choke in the middle of geometry class (as a joke of course). When the oxygen finally galloped back to my brain my first thought was *it felt so nice to be held so closely by a boy,* even if he wanted to knock me out of shape.

Almost all my best friends growing up were dykes / AGs / butch & my Uncle wouldn't let them sleep in the same room with me, afraid we'd make more disappointments because where we come from, girls that dress like line breaks don't sleep in the same bed as boys who are double entendres because: that's the kind of poetry that can get you killed. & everything feels deadly when you are not taught how to feel. But this one time in my 10th grade Art History class, I climbed onto the table to dance like Ciara did in the 'Oh' video & no one laughed or maybe they did & it sounded like applause. I've always been a performer, I just didn't want to become history.

That sophomore summer I spent a lot of time on Limewire looking for videos I could masturbate to & I got curious - or maybe the truth wanted to set me on fire. One time, my cousin caught me near-orgasm at the family computer but I quickly managed to turn the screen into a wormhole & all my family got swallowed into the void (in me) because being caught with my pants down was better than being caught wanting to be free. By junior year, poems were not enough & I was fucking my way to an addiction trying to kill something or someone in me. The lesson being: all wars start with dick. That wormhole still gnawed at my head it seemed, until my mother would launch out the other side & every woman I had been with & all the boys I wanted to be with had her eyes.

By the end of junior year I had left so many bodies strung up under the stairwells & bleachers & parking lots like debris lost in space. I grew so depressed when their bodies couldn't mother me back into a poem or a slice of oxygen. All of senior year was a blur. The liquor started taking over. Things weren't adding up. So I came up with equations to wear on my body so no one would ask questions or smell the clumsy grief warring within me.

Years passed, and I returned to perform at my old high-school. All the memories flooded me like the sting of going cold-turkey. I make a living off of my poems now & I'm not such a fan of math anymore but so much that made me who I am started in the echoes of this building. I can't help but feel stuck somewhere between gratitude & shame, encouraging everyone to be out of this world when I am still in a battle to be myself. All I see in the auditorium are seats filled with secrets, curious pupils & satellite ears hungry for all of my shapeshifting stories. I suppose in many ways, I am still not free & it doesn't make sense like trying to solve all my math problems with metaphors.

A BRIEF TIMELINE OF SORROW

PANTOUM OF MY SECOND SUICIDE ATTEMPT AS INTERSTELLAR PLAYS IN THE BACKGROUND OF MY HOTEL ROOM

I asked a star how to die beautiful.
& the mourning poured out a constellation from a pill bottle
all of the different colored moons danced in my head &
down my throat, until I dreamt a quiet galaxy

& the mourning poured out a constellation from a pill bottle
euphoria is my life on a sentence
down my throat, I unquiet the dream into a galaxy
where I tell no one, so they don't see the void I've become

euphoria, is my body on a life sentence
I beg the sky to make me celestial, full of growing things
where I tell everyone, so they can see the void I've become
the audience for the sunless planet unable to escape my mind

& I learned to make myself still. bright. alive even. on a stage
the pills ask: how does a star die, beautiful?
the audience only wants suns, not the planets I can't escape
with all the different colored moons still dancing in my head

ELEPHANTS

You are not as tired of the poem as I am of the memory
- Jericho Brown

I remember the night
the day?
I remember the long walk home
no, it was the bus ride?
I remember the weight
how light?
I remember your fault
was mine?
I remember the bed
the floor?
I remember the second
not the first time?
I remember his smell
her snake fang?
I remember the unsettling dust
the poison shadow?
I remember the friend
the lie I told myself?
I remember the quiet
mouse in my brain?
I remember arms herding me
hurting me?
I remember
???????
I remember the questions
shame carries in the eyes
I remember asking for it
to stop?
do you remember?
I wish you were a stranger?
you do remember
am I still unforgettable?
I remember the long knife
why do you curse me so?
I remember the truth

like blood & bone?

I remember the strangeness

a lingering haunt of years?

I remember the songs

I can no longer listen to

I remember the way _____

you scuttle in all my dark?

TRAUMA DICTIONARY (10-14-17)

[1]**phan·tom jam**...noun...

1: when dense traffic crawls to a halt due to breaking unnecessarily, causing a domino effect...also... believing said traffic is due to:

a) accident and first responders
b) bad weather
c) construction

[2]**phan·tom jam**...noun...

1: when your mother called after our bodies crashed into each other in the Texas heat of a one-night stand, said you were under construction

2: when I found out you weren't biologically mine almost four years later - on accident - the dominos began to fall for an unnecessary break filled with lessons:

a) heartbreak is always closer than it appears
b) hurt people hurt only themselves

[3]**phan·tom jam**...alternative noun...*AMBIGUOUS GRIEF*

1: *the act of grieving the death of a loved-one who is still alive due to:*

a) all the years I thought I'd have to watch you grow
b) loving you until my father's carcass fell from my shoulders

example 1:
what is a death with no grave to visit, no ashes to scatter?
example 2:
this poem, a haunting in metaphor saying *I miss you*

[4]**phan·tom jam**...alternative noun...*VASECTOMY*

1: The first time I lost a child was a miscarriage.
2: The second, a failure to merge
3: You were the charm, and I am a cemetery of want
I cannot bear to offer ghosts to anyone else
4: there are so many ways to parent; children are not a seance to bring back a dead thing...*or*...mechanics to fix our traumas (see alternative noun AMBIGUOUS GRIEF)

[5]**phan·tom jam**...*transitive verb*...**1 a** *(1) HURTING (2) SHAME (3) GASLIGHT (4) RESENT*

1 b when you finally accept it's better to be under construction than to rush into another broken home

example 1:

my therapist asks: *"how are you doing, today?"*

a) I'm fine
b) I don't know
c) I am not my father
d) I'm still stuck in traffic

LAZARUS

my mother calls
me to say my father is dying
& with tongue heavy as a tombstone
I spill a memorial service

I am no savior, mama.
if you don't sow into your seed
you are only going to harvest

nothing
has changed. I am still the mortician
of his absence & here I am again,
calling my father dead
before the dying is complete.

yes, I too kill my parents in my poems:
a quiet murder masked in healing
for all the times his ghosting
left me feeling like a bad harvest
unworthy of his remembering

I am no savior, mama,

just guilt clawing its way out of years
of silence buried in the back of my throat
somedays, I can't tell if this dirt is mine or

that of a man who moonlights
as a wisp of smoke?
who only reaches for fatherhood
now that the crows circle?

asking his Cancer to heal him
while his cancer kills him,
maybe there's always been bad blood
between us

I am no savior

nor seance
just a child who does not know
how to mourn the undead.

KICK / PUSH – AN ERASURE FOR THE MISCARRIAGE

First didn't know

matter fact

landed

for a week? had to

END right here

shorty was something

so appealing

He couldn't fight something about

he couldn't

since the first kick

cucump cucump cucump

couldn't stand it

banished in the morning

after

said *I'm sorry young man there's no here*

So push push

away with no place to

kick

and be

and

My man got a little older

end up killing him

what momma said

a little more

she was

Love what was happening

said *I would* but

don't think (this) *is strong enough to carry two*

said

I *need*

him

she said

I'm sorry *no*

kick push

away with no place to go

push

for a place to be

push

he had

spitfire and

push no more

wasn't safe no more

wasn't getting no more

breathing

to escape out

things got crazy needed to break

with the world

until the

kick

without a place to

push coast

with me looking for (your)

kick

A GHAZAL IN WHICH THE BOY LOOKS IN THE MIRROR AND WEEPS.

Trying to tilth the soil of my childhood washed in the flood
to say I am more than just emptiness; I am enough.

Swallowed by the longing money cannot change
lost friends, lost lovers, lost time – death has had enough.

What didn't kill me made me more lonely,
maybe the liquor will help when *love* is not enough?

I am grieving the person I thought I would be.
before disappointment's greedy hands have enough.

Success is immaterial when it cannot fix your brokenness;
it was not your fault. it is not my fault. Now rest. enough.

DROWNING AS A MAGIC TRICK

i.

the pledge

the magician shows you something ordinary:

like a deck of cards,

a bird,

a poem–

asks you to inspect it

is it real? normal? alive?

are you watching closely?

sink

ii.

the turn

The magician takes the ordinary thing and makes it do something extraordinary

: ABRACADABRA :

(means functional depression is the turn you never see coming

the performance of swallowing swords in order to spit out flames

but pretty words only do so much when the applause

doesn't come home with you. My brain turns my body

into a water tank coffin for the moments I despise

being in my own skin or on a stage because everyone

looks at PAGES, but no one ever sees / me

- drowning.   *grief makes you grow gills*

My therapist asks – how are you today?

The-world-is-I-is-everybody-is on fire

(but everything is fine?)

my smile is a trap   *door*

of

the

strong

friend

hanging

on

by

an

invisible

thread

I am ████████████████████

forced to become a vanishing act in order to stay alive

buried so far under

man the fuck up | pray harder

don't you know what doesn't kill you

makes you believe

the trauma inside of your own body is not indeed real:

Today: I drank so much I became addicted to the fire, proof I could not burn

Tomorrow: do you eat or keep a roof over your head?

Yesterday: I was sexually assaulted as a child & my mother found out from my poem going viral on Youtube 15 years later. She did not want to believe that it was indeed real, because then how could she I, be normal?)

(Go in, poet!

You on fire poet!

Spit that fire, poet!

Don't be nice, be nasty!

You killin' em, dead poet!

You cuttin' up, poet!

Burn the house down, poet!

You are still on fire, poet

You're bleeding, poet

You aren't breathing, poet

You are made of smoke, poet

Are you watching closely?)

see, how the fire can turn back into a sword?

iii.

the Prestige

you can't just make it disappear,
you have to bring the ordinary thing back

depression is indeed real – but suffering is not normal

I pledge to cry, to let go, to fight for this healing

one resurrection day at a time

the real magic is when the voices

are not louder than the people who love you

especially on those days when you do not love yourself.

ain't that extraordinary?

to stretch your mouth wide as your own undoing

I have to come back,

you HAVE to come back,

I will always come back

: ABRACADABRA :

MANY TINY REVOLUTIONS

II. SPOILED CHILD LEARNING AMERICA'S ENGLISH

Part 2. Information About You (continued)

Your U.S. Mailing Address

I was once a house full of stories:

Almost all of them for this American dreamin' and the last one is me, still trying to translate the catacomb accents of my parents' tongues when they would say: you have become so American now. I know what they mean is deport all of that tribe from your mouth you talk like them now / you walk like them now / No more of that Yaoundé stuck in your teeth, now everything tastes like the steps to unbirthing a country which is to say America, has a way of killing everything that it comes from.

Other Information

I learned early how to fold myself into a flag. I stitched myself a newly striped name - a new set of stars. I was always able to pass through customs, but

my tongue had to stay behind.

U.S. Physical Address

a passport can feel like

a smooth stamped death sentence.

Your Country or Countries of Citizenship or Nationality

List all countries where you are currently a citizen or national. If you need extra space to complete this item, use the space provided in **Part 6. Additional Information**.

A memory?

Too Black for Africans and too African for Blacks?

A meaningless story of anti-Blackness in America.

A name thick in chemically-enhanced amendments,

Wishing for a white picket flesh while living with Section-8 bones.

Part 2. Information About You (continued)

Place of Birth

List the city/town/village, state/province, and country where you were born.

You can be a house,
but America has a way of reminding you
that you are not a home.

Not even inside of your own body.

You are only the debris;
the aftermath;
the constant reconstruction;
the projects redlined in grief;

Information About Your Eligibility Category

They will say that you don't belong in the country that
doesn't even belong to itself

Information About Your Last Arrival in the United States

Oh, america ...

Show us your papers. Who documented your dream? How has it become mine?
Where the attack dogs can still smell the unalienable right from my brittle & marginalized skin

I know the bullet does not care which side of the ocean I am from
it will swim thru my body all the same
it will try to make a home of me until my name is but a salted exit wound

But I know my tongue is still patiently awaiting my return

Yet I wonder
if I will still feel like a stranger in my own house

or

like a language
that is always worth coming home to.

12 DISCIPLES FOR ALL MY NIGGAS

after tafisha a. edwards

All my Niggas is Gods.
All my Niggas is God's.
But no one believes them.

is God all Nigga? My, my,
My Niggas, Gods's all, is
No one to believe in.

My Niggas be all: Goddamn!
All my Niggas, is. But don't
believe they got God in 'em.

GOD
god?
Dieu
Baba
Deus
Domini
Seigneur
Almighty
Dollar Dollar Bill Y'all
Father
Yahweh
Adonai

All my Niggas is Gods
All my God is Nigga,
my God, my God. Buh' lee dat.

THEY	//	HE
all masculinity begins with	//	masks
longing to be more than the grief	//	forgotten
that ties a string around gender. I am	//	torn
between that nigga & that bitch & that	//	*bitch-ass nigga*
broken child stewing in their own	//	understanding
inherited suffering for	//	good blood
rocket worship. let the church say	//	a "man"?
in the name of queerness dressed in	//	a craving
denial. the frothy want to be	//	desired
seen. to be brave (may be?) or just left	//	alone
to remember the days I'd rather just be	//	alive

THE ROPE REMEMBERS THE CRIMSON RECORD

For Trey Reed and all the ones who did not come home.

the first time I held a neck
this tight, I turned his breath into doves –
McIntosh, first of his name –
you smile like he once did
before he crackled for a thousand eyes

I remember back before I became
this American amnesia that necklaces the heart of the wailing

I'm sorry,
do I...know you?
you seem so familiar...

what year is it?
you say hung himself?
but I am covered in so many fingerprints
suicide is a curious name for ku klux
& daddy's bail money stiff as the body
so Black it's blue, with police investigation all over

Trey Reed is your name?
"Reed" as in a tall, slender grass which grows
in water or on marshy ground
& they ain't never let nothing grow on a Mississippi swamp
when the grass ain't always nigger on the side
but I swear you seem so familiar
with all that whistling in your blood
like children the color of a harvest
a spectacle of seeds that grow in any sky
or high school gymnasium
or vacation with a group of "friends"
or traffic stop fed to the hungry mouth of a body cam
we are all watching the feed

Trey, I hate this blooded bond we share
this humidity between us
this vile suffering of bad apples
spoiled by gravity
I held them all just like you,
I am afraid I will hold many more as they slip in and out of time
like seedlings growing into postcards;
like knees to a neck;
like trying to see the forest for the family trees

did you know, the earliest ropes were made of reed?
what a cruel irony to be related by a need to survive

how can they say it was such a long time ago
when all the timelines blur like a tomorrow
stuck in the aching belly of 146000 yesterdays?
when the lynchings ain't never stopped?
they only grew shinier teeth & hungrier stomachs
they want you to forget ...forget...forget...
over it

I'm sorry
do I...know you?
you seem so familiar...

what year is it?

IMMIGRATION & CUSTOMS ENTOMOPHOBIA OF THE "TOXIC BEAUTY"

We, *the rainbow milkweed locusts,* take all of the poison
fed to us, forge it into gorgeous armor.

see me: the tired & poor, huddled into masses. But I know
your constitution as pesticide too

Farm the lifeblood of this hive. Caught in the anthem of plagues:
the business of deportation & children for crops was

your intent. The bone of this wild country is my Aunties
fueling it's very american dream, as we yearn in ahistoric

more than just a buzzing nuisance in the flag's veins.
a country fluent in war, only knows how to other

your entomophobia swarms into a suffering: *they*
are infesting our land & eating our harvest.

Because the prettier something is, the more dangerous.
Who knew my colorful passport would make me a toxic beauty too

or bear a legacy of fathers filled with ghosts? The dirt won't
change the soiled body. When you raid us, it's spray first

ask for humanity: never. Skin is just another wall, didn't
you know? The border of cruelty & a frothy want

to take, & take, But I learned resurrection to take back
all this pretty covered in the spices you stole and don't use

makes america ugly again, a nation of predators - proud
anthems from sea to shining red sea. We will bite every hand.

For the ones who survived the stinger of ocean and desert
who became the rotting, just so their children get to be fly

YA'ARBURNEE*

a golden shovel from a lyric in "Dear God" by The Roots

flip the script / 'murrca, got bible belt wrapped around its arm injecting another mass shooting / why?
cuz Jesus rhyme with guns / the right to bear arms *is* a trap / but the right to bear children / *is*
not / too much to ask? to want them to grow up long enough to dance with daffodils / instead the
hope is in the bullet wounds at their hands & feet / for proof of their AR-crucifixion / in a world
that got an addiction to murder / they say it's all in 'murrca's God given rights to protect its ugly,
purchased for the low price of smallpox & cotton & 4 little girls & Hip-Hop / but, when
'murrca got bad habits called police & politicians, artificial imitation would like you
to swallow small lead bodies & your own blood / a chalk outline communion made
in remembrance of their paid leave / a dogged ruthlessness & savagery / isn't it
a crime? to want to make it home for supper   (not the last one) in
time for my lover to say: *God, we give thanks for your*
child, and the BANG! that wasn't made in their image.

TRANSMOGRIFICATION SPELL BEFORE THE RENT GOES UP

with a sample from Chuck Brown

in the name of *it don't mean a thing if it ain't got that Go-Go swing.* in the name of the children, the homies, the hood, & all the ghosts. in the name of being at home & alive before & after the streetlights come on; before & after the duwop duwop duwop duwop. hear me out now: the sunrise is a promise to turn your wounds into lush moons; your heart loud as blunts forcing trauma out of the body.

may the duwop of Black Mommas & their chocolate city smile like Benning Road before the Starbucks grew teeth. may Duke Ellington's trumpet cough up the southside & Marvin Gaye's voice choke the vacant skylines out of Barry Farms. may the pale plague of thieves who throw stones from their chic glass empires be haunted by Chuck Brown's guitar.

ain't the tree still beautiful even after its limbs gave birth to a swollen pome? ain't the ocean still glimmer & waves despite the wild dream bottom? if the answer is *hallelujah,* then, may the only thing dripping red from the meat be mumbo sauce. may the ohm of popped gum laughter & swinging Black girl locs be a speak-in-tongues majesty you cannot steal or mugshot. may the body bag have an upset stomach & give all of my Niggas back.

AT MY BROTHER'S WEDDING, MY AFRICAN ASS AUNTIE ASKS ME: "WHY DO YOU PAINT YOUR NAILS?"...

...as if to really ask: *what kind of gay are you?* All of them. The worst kind. The best kind. The *abeg, Auntie, you need to fix that ugly ass weave on your head and stop askin' stupid ass questions* kind. The sassy grenade murdered in broad daylight and won't make the news kind. The, *we always knew* but hoped for a false alarm kind. The "this is what happens when there ain't no real man in the house" kind! But another one of my students, living with a "real man" of a father and a Black eye for a mother, fashioned their necks into haute couture and left blood all over their 16-year-old runway. I too was almost a casket's next top model, but I became the better-late-than-dead-bolted kind. So, since ya wanna be Ms. Fox News, all up in my business, my pronouns are Zelle, Venmo, Cashapp/ pay me for all this labor cuz, *BITCH, HAHA! IS YOU MAD?! CUZ MY PUSSY POPS SEVERELY AND YOURS DON'T*?! You think I'm going to hell? Awww. Imma look good dancing all the way there like hol' up, aint that YOU?! I recognize that UGLY ASS WEAVE ANYWHERE! I mean are you OKAY?! If you hate me just say that! Ain't got shit to do with Jesus. He is the only Black man who loves my halo of wool without needing to bleach all of this holy. No, Auntie, even if I got married, it would be a no one here would come to my wedding kind. Y'all better not come to my funeral either. You're probably the reason why I am dead anyway. All of your shame you want me to inherit as you fix your loaded mouth to ask me about my nails before you ask if I unswallowed the pills today. If being alive doesn't feel like a burden today. The days my gender and sexuality want to be safe more than I want to be brave. You more worried about which hole I'm in to see if it's wide enough for your "imaginary man" to step through? You more worried about "body parts", rather than that Uncle who touches the children at every family reunion? You more worried about the sin that I am not, rather than making an effort to see the God in me. So yes I am attracted to him, & her, & them, & maybe if someone told you that you were stardust you wouldn't be threatened by how I shine as I just try to fast forward to the good part. Do my Niggas even get a good part? Where we don't gotta wear armor; become switchblades; choose between queer or Black at every family function side-eye, every snake-eyed fetish; every barbwire police or politician who makes a choice for us while choosing us in secret cuz they love how we make them cum as hard as Marsha P Johnson's brick. But I'm the illegal in 31 out of 54 African nations, kind. That means I'm the I can't even go home, kind. The *leave me alone please* but don't leave me, kind. *Auntie I know your kind...*

...The "do you know where your husband is?" Kind.

TONGUES AS CASTING NETS

There are 16 different stages in the life cycle of shrimp from egg to adult:

Egg
portuguese explorer fernando po & I have one thing in common:
we both love shrimp

Nauplius
when my country emerged from the mesh of his mouth
- his tongue a casting net - he named us after his hunger

Camarões, or *land of shrimp,*
after its abundance found in our River Wouri.

in 1884, Kamerun was first colonized by the germans
war gives so many bodies

example: in 1916, germany lost the 1st world war; Cameroun
became the heart of Africa given to france & britain to rule

with a split tongue anthem: *chant de ralliement*
the rallying cry / of a country singing colonization with pride

Protozoea
language gives so many bodies
example: in 2018, the english conflict with the french-speaking

when you eat shrimp you have to separate shell / from meat
- pick it apart, carefully, from the head

example: Mile 16, once a thriving neighborhood in my capital
now littered in shell casings / picked apart from headshots

<u>*Mysis*</u>
we have more indigenous languages than species of shrimp
yet we fight over whipped tongues turning us shells of ourselves

fact: *the pistol shrimp's explosive attack mimics a gunshot*
fact: *doctors will often leave a bullet in if caused infection*

Cameroun is the internal organ, language is the bullet
there is always an infection

<u>*Postlarva*</u>
food gives us so many bodies
example: my lover is allergic to all shellfish.

centuries of explosive attacks from my blood to our dinner plates
every time my stomach growls, all my tongues are in conflict

<u>*Juvenile*</u>
tchaseu si ne zeuzo zou / bless your food before you eat
I make Gumbo or N'dolè for one. I swallow the bullet

<u>*Adult*</u>
the infection has spread to my passport
history gives us so many bodies

THE BONES I MADE OVER THE SUMMER IN FLORITEXAFORNIA

MISSING YOU AT 30,000 FEET

I am on a plane wishing I could live
in every sky if it means being closer to

you.

SAXOPHONE

after years begging my brother for a saxophone
he comes home with a box saying *here is your instrument*

opened the gift, it was a...
clarinet

ever since, it feels like life has been handing me more
clarinets than saxophones

when I opened you, I did not expect a clarinet
pushed over the edge then blame God for not giving me wings

to face the inequalities of your past, factoring both sides
of your pain and distrust to solve for all your exes

the bad decisions, the unnecessary heartaches,
the boundless grief, the reason our favorite song tastes bitter now

I am another rusted note, an empty resonator, a music sheet
of relationship ghosts, the wrong wind

instrument, doesn't take your breath away, it sings the reasons
I do not like buying flowers for the ones I love:

to offer a soon dead thing to show you cherish someone?
what cruel irony, like trying to read you with no ligature

my chest is a box, in it a saxophone pumping
hoping to become instrumental heart,

rather than a love that settles
for what it never wanted.

YOU GON' LEARN TODAY (ABOUT THIS LOVE)

for Phán

my love is curry goat, peanut stew, fried plantains & Jollof
it is a feast & deserves to be feasted on today

my love unfires the gun, un-nooses the rope
it is an undying forest of many loud & joyous mouths

it is a negro spiritual wrapped in a trap song,
a revolution that grew up to become a Yaaaaaaaaaaaaas

& loved all of its stones & walls so fiercely
it is an amen worthy of any mouth

my love is the countless named & unnamed who swallowed
all of the darkness & spit out a rainbow of cannot be fucked with

my love be depressed sometimes, be so hurt sometimes
my love needs niggaz to go to therapy

my love is like damn...I AM NIGGAZ
my love is a soft nigga, a hood nigga,

my love loves my niggas, & it's only for niggas
for so long who were told they weren't worthy of being loved back

my love is always fine, my love is always good
even when it knows it ain't cuz my love got trust issues

my love knows my peace way too important to turn into bad news
so my love prays for you. keeps a blade for you.

my love be a trumpet & sings for you.
says let's go jump out of a plane & let the clouds carry the burdens

my love from around the way.
way back where time only exists when we wish it to.

my love is so grateful that you are still alive.
that you chose to glide through the thick syrup of circumstance

even when everything turned into a bitter riot.
even when everything said war would be sweeter.

my love says dance, like we are one nation under a groove,
like we release the shame because it was never ours.

my love is machete-mouthed, finally learning how to slay
my love is a gotdamn that knows it's got something to say!

LOVE LOOKS IN THE MIRROR AND SEES GRAVITY

I.

Love is a natural phenomenon by which all physical bodies attract each other. Love gives weight to physical objects and causes them to fall toward the ground. The theory of relativity describes love as: "a consequence of the curvature of space/time."

I fell for you

relatively speaking

the morning after, filled with thousands of light years between us

each a reminder of every curvature of you that sprung me into heat

I thought we were in gravity once

turns out I was inconsequential, a theory that couldn't wait:

now, I'm just a Pluto that you used to know

II.

Love is responsible for planets orbiting the sun as the dominant force which causes the shape and trajectory of astronomical bodies.

We used to listen to *"drops of Jupiter"* whenever we fell out of orbit. to remember what it is like for gravity to flourish between us. To not go to bed angry. To clean up after our solar system. To see the fault in our stars & say *I still want this with you.*

But every sun eventually dies.

III.

Love has no direct impact on sound.

there is no sound in space
there is so much space between us

VI.

Gravity is a complex emotion that can refer to a feeling of strong affection, care, and respect for another person.

I was in gravity with an Armageddon of whiskey
& rough sex. The most beautiful Scorpio who
Gemineyed me until we became the same blue/
black of lonely & bad decisions.

My fifth, fourth, & third gravity
were promises for a universe that would not collapse.
I didn't know how to love myself
without believing everyone ends up floating away
when they couldn't make my scars rhyme.

But when I felt it for the first time,
it was a blackhole.
maybe you were still waiting for me on the other side?

I don't know how to let go

this lifting curse of the heart, this floater's penance
wondering where did our gravity take us
that we returned so far from ourselves?

THE ANATOMY OF WORSHIP

it takes twelve facial muscles to produce a smile
disciples spreading the gospel of your pulse
once thomas-tongued, until you saw
-ed me in half and poured a soft gospel out of me

I take off my shoes before I enter you
this is how we pray, mirrored hands & wine lips
turn me into a lamentation, turn back to the water
baptize the breath, let them rise like an Amen

MY EX USED TO SAY I WAS THEIR FAVORITE PIANO

But now I just open
my stomach and
show the metamorphose
of butterflies into sour notes
a mouth can be made of chords
progressing, swallowed by the keys
held by the one who makes you
beg for fingers
that may glide the throat
and unlock many soft songs.

CHORUS FOR THE SLAUGHTERHOUSE

My last love was blood on a chopping block

I wanted softness, hoping you'd put down the blade

You wanted an unknowing lamb

My heart was a cutting board taking all the damage

So you could make meals for someone else.

Loving you taught me to beware the sound of metal.

UNICORN

is
what he
calls me, I am
prettier as something
that doesn't exist, until I
become his favorite compass.
my mouth a map leading him out
of the parts of him he buries; the parts
only my hands & teeth can unearth; I turn
from legendary creature to just beast. a tongue
never forgets how the touch is an angle to every me-
-mory phantom. he loves all of my lines, the ways they
haunt him. I become a shape before someone he can love;
he leaves me a gift folded as neatly as his envy to be an open
truth rather than a secret, searching for himself in my eyes as he
moans for direction before he closes the door. his trail of bills are
breadcrumbs in case he ever gets lost again & whoever said time is
money must've forgot 'bout love I mean just imagine how cruel the
world must've been to make them forget. what else is my body but

distance

GOD IS A MOTHER WHO DIDN'T GET TO BE A CHILD

THE BOY'S COLLECTION OF MOTHERS

my fourth mother
is a God fearing vinyl /needle touching
itself, Anita Baker & Holy Ghost sampled into a fever
pitch. brass knuckle to glass jaw

my middle school
mother is a bone in my mouth,
a razor's edge contemplating the skin,
stubborn absolution

my high school mother is a shareable link
a watering hole, cradle of hands staining
my mouth - I was a youthful prey.

my adolescent mother
was a praying one. more afterthought for most
days, a bitch: half bite / half
slow dance in the middle of any room

my current mother is the most beautiful man
I have ever met.

my last mother will be messy
bad motherfucker / shard of thunder ready
to pierce flesh
& make it easier to forgive

the madness

my first mother is the flood & the ark
she washes over; she makes things new
she tries, she tries, she tried...

just wasn't enough.

ON A CONVERSATION WITH MY MOTHER, SHE NOTICES MY WOLF RING

nice guys are wolves in
well-tailored wool. Their prettiest & polite
teeth,   hide the most flesh
stained in a respectable death
-     your father killed me
with his kindness - his soft
smile sharp as a carnivorous howl
ready to make a home out of
any thing willing to be the hoofed
& the blood. To be a transmutation
of disappearances,
convinced   me, I
was   crazy, that straightjacket is
better than truth: love by
gaslight - tip the oil, spark the fire
he would burn the entire forest
just to hide the evidence
of clawed tracks soiling the
earth, until our entire family was just a throat
full of ash, I wore my silence so loudly
his wool taught me to be a costume of hushes
I don't think he ever saw himself further than this
ache; than the stories beneath the bruise;
than this addiction to pretty —
it still hurts, no matter how soft the blow is.

AFTER ANOTHER CONVERSATION WITH MY MOTHER, I TRIED TO CALL THE FRESH PRINCE OF BEL AIR TO FIGURE OUT IF WE HAVE THE SAME FATHER...

...then the next morning I woke up with bruises on the inside of my mouth. There was so much blood, I mistook it for a family reunion. This is how I learned the guilt eating at the generational roots of all my parts until all that's left is a father like *Lou*.

Did you know *Loup* is also the French word for wolf? The universe loves its jokes. Like the cruelty that once sat at my mother's door with a violent gnaw for a kiss. For years I watched her bear a moon- sized lump inside of her throat where all of my father's lies

got caught as she swallowed her pride & he transformed. The new-minted beast wears wolf well, chewing at her fairy tale heart. She kept crying: *wolf, WOLF!* But everyone said __________ & this world is so good at its silence & protecting its boys, it forgets about

its daughters eaten alive until they become unrecognizable. The boys never seem to remember *WHY HE DON'T WANT ME, MAN?* Never seem to remember the bruises they leave behind who grow up bloody. Or that they were once a belly's lump too.

I GREW MY HAIR AS A PROMISE TO THE BOY

my momma wants me
to be Jonah, get swallowed
by all of her
traditions that came from a
colonizer's hand with
centuries of whip-swing calluses
she'd rather me alive
in the belly of the beast
than dead in the ocean
of my kinky rebellion.
I promise, I only
look like something you don't
understand because
you think there is only
loss here. check out my
new-growth, conjured slick
wave who knows their name;
mama, I braid it! I promise,
I won't turn you
to stone

I promise.

MARITIME IN LOUM

My grandmother Mami N'toung was a seashell.

The first time I ever visited our muddy village of Loum,
she searched for my mother in my face,
hoping my eyes would be a lighthouse guiding to a safe shore:

Womeule?
            Womeule?
                        Womeule?

At six, I was still understanding the ocean of our mother-tongue,
but her salt was enough to birth a translation.
When she could only find my father in my face,
she grew into tired waves:

I was a bad decision, ruin-reminder
mistake she didn't want to be forced to love;
Her eyes swarmed with sharks smelling the feast
of unfamiliar blood, how she quickly reverted to her shell...
when all I ever wanted was to be her favorite pearled
grandchild without expiration.

did you enjoy our time with Mami N'Toung?
I coughed up water for an answer.

My grandfather passed away two weeks
after our visit. Some say he died of old age,
rumor is he got caught
in all of her undertow.

'Til this day when I think of Mami N'toung,
all I can do is hold my breath.

I GOT FAMOUS OFF MY POEM ABOUT BEING RAPED GOING VIRAL & RESENTMENT BE LIKE...

when your mother asks you about the poem

lie. tell her it was just something you wrote, just another day of
making my living out of my nightmares. of learning how to hold my
reflection less like an arranged marriage. for the first time

you will know a deep & visceral courage. how to become the levee
that wishes for a different life. or the day you grew a deep hatred til
your blood angered to a razor spill & two bouts of addiction

your family still doesn't know about. how you swore to be nothing
like the violent ghost your father was. tell her you were brave, that
you made anvils of your hands & you are still the ~~man?~~ she raised

*

when the stranger at the show asks how have you come this far?

I sow my skin into kevlar; I go for morning walks;
I watch way too much crunchyroll; I don't know.

*

when your mother asks have you prayed to God to forgive...?

where the fuck you been at, God? I read your bible, I spat your
prayers. I've seen your miracles of fire-flowers & parted seas

where were my locusts to devour her flesh away from mine?
where was my rain of fire to burn his fingerprints from my bones?

after turning to wine for so many nights, drunk on my depression
I wonder if my mother meant them or me?

*

when your partner doesn't ask you about the poem

& you know you both share an unforgiving // history of assault
you will learn a different kind of silence
how it is a heavy thing // bursting at the seams with hallelujahs

allow the clumsiness of your hands to process, know that you will
make mistakes // there will be hurt there too
but your body is not a lie, let the truth of every scar bury you

in the anthem of moans // you've made a weapon of your body for
too long already. they don't need you to be sword
nor shield // a lover's kiss, gentle shipwreck, tender aftermath

*

when you ask yourself...

*

when your mother doesn't ask you about that poem

undo the locks around your throat
tell her of the love after the breaking
tell her of the boy
tell her you are the poem with much editing to do.

WE PLAYED SADE & WHITNEY HOUSTON ON SUNDAYS

because *I'm Your Baby Tonight* was more than just a classic
it was a call to arms –shoulders, knees, & floating feet
cushioned in her favorite house slippers,
the fancy ones that glittered like a Bikutsi sermon
how beautiful my mother looked in her oil-stained dress as she
twirled to the sonic anthem unbuckling her hips & the bass
massaging the plastic off the sofa with not a single spill from her
glass full of grown-up juice flying between her fingers, even
the mop knew to glide to the sloshy beat & i barely understood
English at the time but my body just knew *Diamond Life* is
what happens when God transcends language & logic leaves
the room unburdened for once because what good is
knowing without feeling & memory is a motherf*@#er
& now i miss my momma, how we used to trip the light like
orchids & it's been a while ; *i should call her more, huh,* but i
have another show to get to & i just missed my exit jamming
so hard to this playlist of Black womxn with voices that sound
like what the universe must've Blues'd like when it was being made
& there's so much music in my head, now
i'm twice the incompetent child but at least i still clean on sundays.

THE PH BALANCE OF PARENTING YOURSELF *

Mother's Love

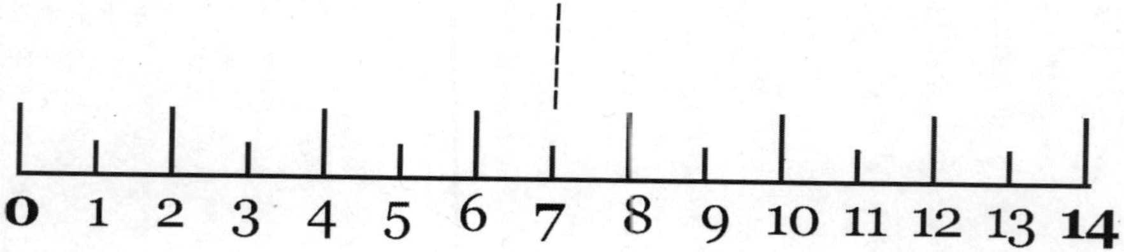

←——**Sadness   Anger***——→

*I am learning not to be the imbalance

**my mother shows up for me in my poems

***the ways she won't show up for me in my life

BAGS UNDER THE EYE OF THE STORM

III. STOCKHOLMED CHILD UNLEARNING

Part 3. Applicant's Statement, Contact Information, Certification, and Signature

NOTE: the **Penalties**
You
Form while in the United States.

either

1.a. ☐ understand English,
and understand

1.b. ☐ every

2. ☐ At request,

6. ☐ if you are
under
settlement

Applicant's

release
may need to
benefit

the
US

if required

ALL APPLICANTS:
submit

THE 2ND TIME I WENT SKYDIVING

I was a giggling tumbleweed out of the airplane
& the Hawaiian sky became the swollen belly of '98:
the last time joy was N'dolè & reruns of Marimar
because that summer, mama didn't work as much

so her two good arms were meant for huggin'
the language out of a little boy's grief
& my sister was still my sister before
a man undressed all his darkness &

laid it at her feet. now her eyes are closets
bursting with too many dingy garments old as
forgiveness & it was too the last summer I saw
my brother before he became a bullet

splashing through the sinewy clouds
of everything that wanted to unmake him
whole; I always wanted to be just like my
brother & look at me now, flying

at the speed of death trying to get free
& all I can think is if God can be drunk
on the job then why can't we?
I mean how else can you explain a mountain

with a spliff in its wide mouth ready
to spit out red hot truth, & oceans
so blue you forget about the sadness? no one
makes a world this beautiful by being sober.

you can't really appreciate the land
until you've time traveled through a sky
full of possibilities & my whipping
memories turn the wind into

all the dead things I hope to leave
behind, before the parachute opens its
longing arms & gives me a chest to lay
all of my blue.

ON A BUS TO TEXAS, I OVERHEAR A PASSENGER SAYING "LOVE IS UNCONDITIONAL"

did you know the jellyfish
is the only immortal creature on earth?

once they've reproduced they do not die but sink
to the ocean floor, transform back into their juvenile polyp state,

now ain't that unconditional?
to know you are always home within yourself

so, maybe I *don't* love you
I immortal jellyfish you.

do you ever wonder what made you possible
in spite of all that wanted to leave you lost at sea?

sometimes I think my mother made the choice
to push me out like a deep sigh

because love is what happens when we fulfill the condition
of letting all of our hurt go.

TATA CAROL

i.

My best childhood memories revolve around her careful slices into the oil, the "love bath" as she'd call it. Treating each one with her wooden spoon hands until they became golden-brown stories. For years before she passed away, I was most fascinated with how she'd turn the blackest and overripe of this not-banana into lessons: those like us, with this Missol'è skin, are not to be thrown away. Surround yourself with, love...bathe in all of its heat. Those of the dark deserve worship too.

i*i.*

So what do you want to eat today? *PLANTAINS.*
Tomorrow? *PLANTAINS.*
The day after tom- - *PLANTAINS!*

The better question: <u>ARE THERE MORE PLANTAINS?</u>

iii.

Keep eating them all the time, you're going to turn into one
-- Tata Carol, the sensible adult.

And I took that personally
-- ME, unsensible, famished child.

iv.
...THE BOY BECOMES THE PLANTAIN AND SPEAKS

You can call me by my indigenous name: Musa Balbisiana, though some call me "Plantin," Patacones, Kelewele, Aloco, or Missol'è, if you're nasty! I am a many-faced God, got over 5000 years of this Maduro munch. You ain't got the Tostones to fuck with me! Can't talk Pilé Pilé to the MofonG.O.A.T.! Yes, I am the GREATEST OF ALL FRIED!10th staple of the world, Tropical dime piece & trans-Atlantic magician. Split me open, & watch me drop this Versace on the floor until I time travel back to

*****M i s s o l' è*****

Born in Southeast Asia, raised in Africa, forced to turn tricks in the Caribbean. cluster-grown, like stars from underground stems rather than seeds. Meaning I am the first strange fruit: the bitter green history of ships and stolen people made ripe with resilience; message from the enslaved: call me ghetto gastronomy; family reunion; Black Indigenous Plantain of Color, mastered how to turn flavor into a map! I am compass, always pointing to freedom. Tell death: HA! I caramelize in the face of danger until tragedy turns into soul food. Ain't that what people of the sun always do?! I am Ogun's first meal: tastes like Harriet's shotgun; I am Mansa Musa Balbisiana; I am the "P" in Huey Newton, swinging Toussaint's machete until Ayiti Cherie submerges massa's oily-hot flesh. Snap! Crackle! HYAH! HYAH! Don't they know the darker the berry, the sweeter the revolution? Never met a mouth – or a death – that WE could not conquer.

v.

see, Tata Carol,
just like how you taught me...

I am what I speak.

MARIO KART UNMAKES ME AN ATHEIST

laughter runs rampant from the cellar of her lungs as I select Pink Gold Peach because Niece Rule #27 clearly states *no one else can have Wario if she has Wario.* we devote hours to the craft of mushroom-powered jumps, Nintendo gods seemingly grant her every victorious wish but on the sticks, I am a petty atheist who doesn't believe in letting kids win no matter how cute their toothless and excited grin is for first place

"next time...", she says with the confidence of a blue shell, "...I swear I will get you next time." and I imagine this is how heaven is made: in the softness of *next time* - a button mash refuge of memories / the tenacious ingredients of family: a recipe we can pass on for generations to undo the Bowsers' godlessness who only speak in fire and throw hammers instead of building bridges; not enough wood to go around, I suppose

the ones who make us small and muted to the touch because it is all about [the] race. I think of rainbow roads like my niece, or my students, or my sequined siblings whose faith is constantly on the chomping block, bullet-billed from who and what they love without any magical clouds to fish them from sea to shining sea. but I want to tell her our family is safe from the storm / that home stretches as far as her tiny hands can reach

stay on track, Wario, yes that's it! you've got this! everything sounds like a lie from a tongue well-seasoned in survival, when the truth slices the throat raw with all its shortcuts. Piranha-planted, too many of us being SNATCHED! maybe that's the idea? the only thing that will bring forth a slow salvation is to lose their coins (because everything is about the coins) or at least that's the altar we are told to kneel to.

maybe, just maybe, we need a little pause. reset. to auto-save this liberation. this high-spirit that makes joy a downloadable content. to not let our lives drift away as her gap-toothed smile reminds me this, is worth fighting for – this, is how the congregation survives; this is how the church has always survived: god is a road of embers, wild-mouthed with possibilities to burn. to rubber. to cannon through any jungle. to last lap Lazarus.

ELEGY FOR THE BLUE SHELL

NooooooooooooooooooooooOooooooooooooooooooooooooooooo
oooooooooOoooooooooooooooooooOooooooooooooooooooooooo
ooooooooooooooooooooOoooooooooooooooooooooooooooooooo
oooooooooooooOooooooooooooooooooooooooooooooooooooooo
ooooooooooooooooooOoooooooooooooooooooooooooooooooOoo
oooooooooooooooooooooooooooooooooooooooooooooooooooooo
ooooooooooooooooooooooooooooooooooooooooOooooooooooooo
ooooooooooOooooooooooooooooooooooooooooooooooooooooooo
ooooooooooooooooooooooooOooooooooooooooooooooooooooooo
OooooooooooooooooooooooOooooooooooooO.

A LOVE LETTER TO EVERY UNION STATION

every neighborhood I grew up on was a bad break up
life had a way of keeping me nomadic
shackled to the wind
of three different continents
a lover's arms
a couch after a long trip on the road
or waiting for a greyhound with just enough
prayers in my back pocket to get home

Union Station, you've welcomed me the most
offered me your crooked benches stained with piss & possibilities
bus & train sounds quilted together
like a warm blanket you'd drape over my distant bones
the myriad of smells – a meal of the city's chatter,

Where were you off to this time?

you are designed to facilitate departures,
yet have taught me most about staying
we've always meshed well
being places of transition
I have moved again -
3rd time in this past year -

I think you'd like it here

ABOUT LIVING AT BAGGAGE CLAIM

Call your inner child // you have them saved in your contacts as *your strong friend* // Congratulate them for how far they've come // Pour yourself your favorite drink // Have that dessert // Learn your apology language // Then, carry no one else's weight // I know you tend to stretch your shoulders // fifty sob stories high & your heart is a country without borders // take all that weight off today // Pluck a wind from the tornado of your past & let it lift you into tomorrow // Get your hair done, nails done, everything did // Then, say thank you to your body // Put that outfit that makes you feel so good even when you have nowhere to go - yes, that outfit that's been collecting years of weight gain & just loss - in the back of your insecurities // Celebrate // getting out of bed //when the gravity of circumstances wouldn't let go // Write that poem. Play that instrument. Paint that canvas. Love again. even if you are bad at it // Ask for help. Trust is in the gift of the unknown // Take that trip you've been meaning to but leave all the baggage behind, especially what is not yours // When you are ready, say *Yes* // Then, rest//Do Nothing // Spend time at the altar of your giggly joy // You don't need another hustle // Quit that job // Cry until you are an ocean of your unmaking // Everything is not happening to you, but much of it is happening for you // You are not alone. It takes millions of years for stars to find their rhythm // You are a universe taking shape.

EPILOGUE: ALL HEARTS ARE OCEANS

ALL HEARTS ARE OCEANS

A short-film in verse

Written by

PAGES Matam

OVER BLACK:

"People think of the word fearless to mean without fear. I see it to actually mean with fear...but you did it anyway." - Luvvie Ajayi.

PRE-LAP: ocean waves in a dreamy undulation.

EXT. BEACH - DAY (DREAM)

THE BOY (10), with skin black as a night bursting with stars, stands at the edge of the sands.

BLAQ (V.O.)
A ndi na sebã, l'anglais linga na titi / Uu lam na mwende anglais n'à muna di pa bol / L'anglais n'est que ma quatrième langue / English is only my fourth language...

The boy looks out into the water, longing.

BLAQ (V.O.)
The baby of the family, the one my mouth spoils favorite by default who may one day be sold off by its siblings in hopes to never return--

The foamy white of waves slowly crashes between his toes...

BLAQ (V.O.)
--all of my other

BLAQ (V.O.) (CONT'D)
tongues have grown so
jealous.

...The giggling Boy notices next to him: an old Magnavox TV.

The relic **CRACKLES ON, hissing from white noise to a 90s cartoon theme song.**

Curious, the Boy turns to the tv and changes the dial.

Another 90s cartoon theme song.

Then another. Then another.

Once he settles on a channel, the Boy dances to the childish sounds. Lost in his rhythms, nothing else matters.

BLAQ (V.O.)
In my country, we have
over 200 dialects.
That's over 200 ways to
say "love". To say
"family".

An EERIE SHADOW shaped like a hand bellows over the Boy's tiny body from behind him, growing larger and larger.

BLAQ (V.O.)
To say "I belong to
something that does
not want to kill me."

The shadow reshapes into a snake's mouth, jaws wide and hungry.

BLAQ (V.O.)
When an ocean of despair crashes unto the shores of your mind, you drown in your own longing.

The Boy, filled with laughter, continues his dance, unknowing of the danger ready to swallow him as the shadow LUNGES!

BLAQ (V.O.)
Grief, makes you grow gills.

INT. BUS - DAY

BLAQ (25), queer west-African poet, a bundle of charm and defiance, snaps awake as the bus ABRUPT-LY STOPS.

His phone playing a video of **Dexter's Laboratory** jerks out of his hand. He picks it up then rises looking out the window.

A sign reads: "OCEANSIDE BEACH, 16 MILES"

Another purple sign next to it reads: "BEWARE - MARINE PESTS"

A whatsapp video call pops up interrupting Blaq's video feed.

It's Blaq's lover, TRU (late 20s), fiercely protec-tive who loves to laugh as much as his adornment of rings.

BLAQ (V.O.)
My lover's voice is an oasis. A reminder that

BLAQ (V.O.) (CONT'D)

every light at the end
of a tunnel isn't an
oncoming train.

Blaq and Tru have an inaudible conversation, all soft eyes and kiss me through the phone. Blaq is so happy to see him.

BLAQ (V.O.)

My heart has always
made me child like.
For the boy - who was
asked to not love
himself.

The bus door hisses open.

Slowly emerging into Blaq's view with steps heavy as time are three FACELESS, armed officers dressed in all-white uniforms with pixelated faces.

Tru grows concerned as a nervous-looking Blaq hangs up.

BLAQ (V.O.)

For the one, who one
day asks to love him.
The one who makes him
feel like a Saturday
Morning Cartoon.

FACELESS 1 approaches Blaq, the lone person on the bus other than the unseen DRIVER.

The Faceless One extends its hand at Blaq who is filled with enough anxiety to make the bus burst at the seams.

Blaq reluctantly hands over a worn-out green

passport.

Faceless 1 scans: IT'S EXPIRED.

BLAQ (V.O.)
Love is knowing why
you are alive.

A mechanical smile spreads from its pixelated face.

All three of the Faceless surge into a **hiss until it skips like a sinister glitchy laugh**.

The seatbelts next to Blaq snake their leathery bodies around him as he fights confused and afraid.

They coil around his neck and torso, tight and unforgiving.

A fruitless fight, Blaq succumbs to his impending fate while the Faceless continue their hissing laugh.

BLAQ (V.O.)
How a single moment
can make the blood of
it all, turn black.

...Blaq sinks into the gaps of the bus seat, as the coiling seatbelts pull him into a darkness.

INT. EMPTY BLACK OF THE BUS

Blaq lands into a pitch black room, strapped to his bus seat.

He now wears a white prison outfit with a single big black question mark at its front and back. He is surrounded by more seatbelts on the ground arranged like a slithering pit of snakes.

Hopelessness slumps his shoulders as Faceless 1 brings him an old rotary phone. Blaq picks up and dials.

Blaq converses with the person on the other line, distraught.

BLAQ (V.O.)
Love is a phone call
from an emptiness you
don't know you will
ever escape. Love is
softening the blow. It
is beginning and end.

He cries, splashed with sadness, then hangs up.

BLAQ (V.O.)
Despair sinks its
teeth into love,
waiting for its moment
to strike and let its
fangs rewrite a story.

Faceless 1 disappears to the front of the bus to the **LOUD CLANK OF A PRISON CELL DOOR RAMMING SHUT.**

INT. EMPTY BLACK OF THE BUS - LATER

Blaq lays cradled in the bus seat like a womb.

Above him a sign flips like **a changing tv dial to a distorted and glitchy 90s cartoon theme song:**

"DAY 1 UNTIL DEPORTATION?"

The subtle sound of waves and children's laughter wooshes in.

Blaq releases **A MUFFLED SCREAM** into the void of the dark.

Blaq clutches his chest, hyperventilating.

A white plastic tray slides into the room next to his face with a paper and a pencil sitting atop of it.

Blaq barely lifts his head up to look, and buries his head right back in.

INT. EMPTY BLACK OF THE BUS - LATER

The sign **glitch-flips**:

"DAY 6 UNTIL DEPORTATION?"

Blaq looks completely dejected, skinny, wearing depression all over his body. He is now surrounded by multiple white trays filled with paper, most of them blank.

Some papers have scratched out words on them: "You deserve this." "This is your fault." "Just give up." "There is no home for you." "Who are you?" "Go back where you came from!"

BLAQ (V.O.)

I was a house once full of stories. One for this American dreamin'. Another for all of the miles of ocean and grandmother's gospels. The last is me, still trying to translate the catacomb accents of my parents' tongues--

Blaq grabs one of the papers, and begins to write.

BLAQ (V.O.)

I am golden child,
born of the dirt.
Hands made of hope. As
American as the apple
pie of their eye,
looking for a sweeter
future.

Blaq writes. And writes. Furiously ripping through one sheet after the other.

BLAQ (V.O.)

No more of that
Yaounde, Cameroun
stuck in my teeth. Now
everything tastes like
steps to un-birthing a
country because Ameri-
ca has a way of kill-
ing all that it comes
from.

Blaq stops writing, looks down in sadness at his bloodied hands smeared on the page.

Blaq, screams inaudibly "LET ME OUT" in a fit of silent rage.

BLAQ (V.O.)

Pleading for noise.
For the silence to
end. Death is so quiet
in the wishing well of
memories.

He tosses all of the papers and creates a flurrying mess.

INT. EMPTY BLACK OF THE BUS - MUCH LATER

The sign **glitch-flips:**

"DAY 9 UNTIL DEPORTATION?"

A naked Blaq, knees to chest, rocks quietly to **the echo of a drop of water like a leaky faucet.**

BLAQ (V.O.)
A paradox of lies. The hiss and bite. The bursting of a heart.

TRU (V.O.)
My heart.

Blaq's head snaps up, as if he has heard his lover's voice, faint in the echoing droplets.

He looks up to locate the voice, a droplet of water leaks unto his face.

Then the leak rapidly increases until it RAINS all over him.

As the water washes over from above, it washes out all of the color in the room, draining at Blaq's barely alive body.

Everything stalls to black and white. The water stops, half of Blaq's body looks submerged giving the image of a fetus.

BLAQ (V.O.)
They will say that you don't belong in the country that doesn't even belong to itself, spoiled child.

INT. EMPTY BLACK OF THE BUS - LATER

The sign **glitch-flips:**

"DAY 12 UNTIL DEPORTATION?"

Blaq seems so small in the bus seat. Colorless. Lifeless.

Just a body wading in the ocean of darkness.

BLAQ (V.O.)
The bullet does not care which side of the ocean I am from. It will swim thru my body all the same. It will try to make a home of me until my name is but a salted exit wound.

Sounds of whooshing waves and child-like laughter permeate the room.

Where Blaq previously laid now is The Boy from our opening, Blaq's younger version, in the same outfit he wore then.

BLAQ (V.O.)
I know a bullet cannot hurt a crashing wave.

The Boy slowly gets up and walks a black corridor, bus windows appear like screens projecting moving images of:

-- Tru and Blaq's first kiss on a fancy dinner date.

-- Their first fight in their apartment.

The Boy picks up the pace and runs as more images appear:

-- Tru and Blaq's first time making love.

-- The first time Blaq shares their immigrant status with a letter marked from US HOMELAND DEPT. Tru hugs Blaq.

-- Blaq on a stage facing a large AUDIENCE as he performs.

BLAQ (V.O.)
My tongue is patiently
awaiting my return.
This body is not a
house I am a stranger
in. I am a language
worth coming home to.

The Boy finally comes to a stop, eyes burning with defiance.

BLAQ (V.O.)
I know who I am.

Those same eyes become Blaq's eyes, as he stands in front of the door of the bus.

Color slowly returns to Blaq, as he reaches to open the door.

BLAQ (V.O.)
I am memory. I am
Blood.

Then the white hand of Faceless 1 grabs his neck from behind, squeezing the life out of him.

Blaq puts up a fight, he uses all of his might to pull away the hand with both of his.

BLAQ (V.O.)
I am water born. I am time and time again.

Then TWO MORE HANDS - Tru's ring adorned hands - join in the fight and help, strengthening Blaq as he pulls away.

BLAQ (V.O.)
I am resurrection.
Born free.

Then TWO MORE hands join them - The Boy's night sky hands.

Blaq wins the struggle and completely pulls away Faceless 1, yanking its hand away then pushing it back!

When Faceless 1 falls back, it takes the form of a WHITE SNAKE, **hissing** at the ready.

The snake bites at Blaq's hand. And bites. And bites. But Blaq just stares it down, like he knows what he must do.

Blaq opens his mouth and stuffs the snake down his throat. He struggles at first but manages to swallow the snake.

Moments later, his hands turn scaly. He sheds his skin, <u>RIPPING AND RIPPING AND RIPPING it off his body.</u>

Until...

The bus door opens pouring out a blinding light.

Blaq emerges graceful, beautiful, ancestral with glittering night skin, a halo of flowers on his head and a large Ouroboros ring on his finger.

BLAQ (PRE-LAP)
Every breath taken is a
love letter to myself...

INT. SANKOFA BOOK STORE - NIGHT

A cozy bohemian book store meets Afrocentric cafe.

An ENGAGED AUDIENCE encircles an older bearded BLAQ (34), adorned with a crown of flowers and still with defiant eyes.

BLAQ
Realizing all hearts,
are oceans.

We realize the narration and fantastical story all this time has been him reading from his book titled: "My Heart Is An Ocean: a detainee's poetry memoir."

A LONG ROUND OF CHEERS AND APPLAUSE fills the intimate room.

TRU (33) is also at front, smiling and in tears.

JAM (34), the warm and super excited host, grabs a seat next to Blaq.

JAM
Wow, from learning
english watching cartoons to N.Y. Times
bestseller!

BLAQ

Stoooop! You're too much. But thank you, Jam! I appreciate you!

JAM

Chile, when we got the news I.C.E. snatched you up at the grey-hound station after our poetry showcase, we were beyond devas-tated. To have you now is such a gift be-cause, girl, I got QUESTIONS!

Everyone chuckles.

JAM

So, why a poetic memoir?

BLAQ

As a kid I used to bother my family to go to the beach every weekend. The water was the only place that reminded me of home, a quiet that made peace more reality than concept. This memoir is my water offering, a conversation on mental health and finding home wherever that may be.

JAM

Period. And you're launching WAVE too?

BLAQ

Yes! The WAVE residency is about empowering Black immigrant and queer artists with tools and support. It's why I got this.

Blaq shows an Ouroboros tattoo on his forearm with a date.

BLAQ

The date I was released. A reminder of gratitude for my community who helped me fight and that no one should live in fear. We all get to get off the bus.

JAM

I know that's right. Speaking of, You think you'll ever go back home some day?

Blaq ponders on the question then gives Tru a long and tender look.

BLAQ

I already am.

FADE TO: BLACK

END SHORT.

button poetry

GRATITUDE & ACKNOWLEDGEMENTS

Thank you to the editors and selection committees for these poems that have appeared in some version or earlier draft in these publications:

Yesterday You tried to call the Fresh Prince of Bel Air to figure out if you have the same father published by Winter Tangerine (2020)

Tongues as casting net published by ROOT Work journal (2024)

Spoiled Child published in Poets.org (2019)

* * *

Parise be to our Ancestors - known and unknown - who continue to watch over us and protect us and bless us.

Praise be to God and all of her indomitable grace.

Praise to the trees.

Praise be to the universe, every atom, molecule, and stardust flowing in this wild cosmos of a heart.

Praise to Palestine. To Congo. To Haiti. To Sudan. To Cameroun. To D.C. To Baltimore. To L.A. To Brooklyn. To Atlanta.

* * *

Home is everyone and every place that I may not remember now, but know that my heart carries you, in all of the light and the heaviness.

Home is Imani Cezanne for every brilliant note, edit, suggestion, cuss out, gentle nudge, and real talk about every line, moment, and purpose.

Home is Ebony Stewart and your vast ocean of a heart; the Gully

Princess, your crown is unmatched and unfuckwitable. Period. They truly cannot handle all your wild geography.

Home is Mrs. Jackie aka Rocky aka my second heart. My infinity. My over 9000.

Home is Lucie, Lauryn, Broderick, and being beyond family. We are soul pillars.

Home is NOVA CYPRESS BLACK & Ziiomi. Y'all make love feel like a wind that can actually be harnessed. Thank you for the storm of laughs, and the warm breeze of this tender friendship. We make rain every time we dance.

Home is Chuck. Aka Chucklandia. Aka Professor X. Aka we siblings for life. In this one and the next. Love you to sobriety and back.

Home is Sarlé, a Deity. A constellation. A breath of fire. A bond beyond bonds. P.S. Zay is dope. Shoutout to your CTRL-V's!

Home is Armel & Ewe. Can't wait for our return.

Home is Tata Carol. Tu me manques beaucoup. Men'de

Home was my mother & father too, and all the mothers and fathers I have collected over the years - knowingly and unknowingly.

Home is NEEN. I adore you and all of your colors. Gang Gang! Splash Splash! I can't wait to see your name on every screen. You give haters a job with a 401K. Keep 'em employed, hunni.

Home is Sherean, the love I didn't know I needed. Illadelph. The rawest to ever do it. We laugh at our pain, then fashion it into the flyest fits.

Home is Ashlee Diamante. Ayiti Cherie. Bone of my petty. Bearer of the dark and the humorous. To Tanzania and back.

Home is Jasmine aka Jazzy Phaeee! I will follow you til the end of time. You are the sunshine of every room. Let's get ramen!

Home is Jasmine O. Fuck a Wednesday. You my every day. My sistah. My dawg. Cheers to more egusi and love island cackles.

Home is Key. I am so grateful for this incarnation of us. Why you take so long, Rodrigo? I can't wait to Alternate Smile with you into our next lifetimes.

Home is Shannan, thank you for making me a better writer, and arguably being one of the dopest human beings to ever craft with. Shoutout to that mighty Pen of yours, it is hella Professional, and kudos for bringing in C-Dawg. You sure know how to pick 'em!

Home is Rudy Francisco, and in all the ways you make poetry and slam more possible.

Home is Gigi my Gigi. You grand spectacle of perseverance. My heart two-steps for you. You have earned your rest. Bread pudding on me.

Home is KaNikki J & 13 of Nazareth, thank you for the warm embraces and curation of joy you always make for me.

Home is Antonio. You the coolest Italian. Thank you for believing in me and taking a chance on me.

Home is Matthew Cuban & Alyesha, I could build mansions of joy out of your hugs alone. Thank you for all the ways you show up and show out. Ball is life.

Home is Phàn. I could spend a 10000000 mondays with you. Here is to 10000000 more.

Home is Phoenix. Arisen from the ashes. Man do you live up to your name. Thank you for being the reason there is even fire in this pen in the first place.

Home is Pic! Ooooooohhh PIIIIIITCHEEEESSS!

Home is all The poetry Giants who have influenced, moved, taught, workshopped, lent an ear or shoulder, or allowed me the honor to witness. It is a privilege to share space with you all:

Droopy, Dwayne Lawson Brown, Sonya Renee, Gayle Danley, Twain Dooley, Patricia Smith. Vievee Francis, Gregory Pardlo, Jericho Brown, Regie Cabico, Angelique Palmer, Rasheed Copeland, Rachel McKibbens, Shihan, Yasiin Bey, Jeanann Verlee, Ashley August, Edwin Bodney, Safia Elhillo, Dominique Christina, Warsan Shire, Dr. Javon Johnson. Eboni Hogan, Denice Frohman, Carrie Rudzinski, Ken Arkind, Ed Mabrey, Joshua Bennett, Iyeoka Ivie Okoawo, Lizz Straight, Queen Sheba, 6 is 9, Theresa Davis, Ashlee Haze, Sierra DeMulder, Janae, Queen Godis, Saul Williams. Andrea Gibson, RADI, & so many gotdamn more. GOSH I LOVE POETRY & POEMS & POETS! DO YOU?

Home is Toni Morrison, Octavia Butler, Ngũgĩ wa Thiong'o, Luther Vandross, James Baldwin.

Home is Anansi & Kirikou. The first stories to mold my imagination into infinite possibilities.

Home is Phenom. I'm still not watching One Piece, bro.

Home is Ainsley Burrows & Laurielle Noel. Thank you for your nurture, for the meals of body and soul, for all of my tears and aches you soothed. For that phone call a decade ago, that literally changed my life.

Home is Sabrina. Suavemente. Flower sparkle. Stubborn earth. I see you. I'm proud of you for all the ways you finally see you too.

Home is Savage, you have taught me so much of what it means to be a truly solid human being.

Home is Rouge, the greatest to ever do it. Swing and dance and fight and murk and SHOW THEM ALL!

Home is Kenneth. Something about you, kid. Building a special ting. Let em go. Your pen is BRIMSTONE and BRICK THROUGH THE WINDOW.

Home is LOC IN! LOOOOAAAD UP!
Home is Maestro, Tomi, Nikki, Celia - YA DOWN WITH OCP!

Home is Spit Dat. Sweet Spot Nation. Beltway. Treat Ya Self. Graffiti DC. Busboys. Da Poetry Lounge. TRIBE. Circle.

Home is Kaleb, Pieume, Nazeer. I will never stop loving you.

Home is my inner-child. Shoutout to you, Apado. We are still alive. And there are so many people who love you and will make a home for you whenever you may need it. You a fly ass kid. Never forget the portal of truth that you are.

To every person reading this book, thank you for giving my words, my creativity, my work ethic a home.

Home is wherever you are.

NOTES

BIRTH CHART AS A CLEAVE
Cancers are water signs, Gemini are air signs, Leos are fire signs, Virgos are earth signs.

CHANGED CHILD LEARNING OF HOME & SPOILED CHILD ON LEARNING AMERICA'S ENGLISH
These poems are written as Hermit Crab challenges, from FRONTIER POETRY Magazine & Publications. The first 2 languages in the first section of "Changed Child..." are *Bamileke* and *Bangk'on*, two indigenous languages to the people of Cameroun, Central Africa. Both poems are part of a series utilizing the i-765 USCIS Employment Authorization form for Immigrants.

PLEASE DON'T LET [THE BOY] BE MISUNDERSTOOD
the title borrows from the song "Don't let me be misunderstood" by the Animals.

IT'S MORPHIN' TIME
The title borrows its name from the popular phrase uttered by characters in Saban's *Mighty Morphin' Power Rangers!*

WAR-TORN
Is after the "Alien Suite" by Safia Elhillo.

BI'S POETICA
This poem is written in the spirit of an Ars Poetica.

ELEPHANTS
This poem is written in the form of a Pregunta. The line with "blood & bone" is borrowed from the book "Children of Blood and Bone" by Tomi Adeyemi.

PANTOUM FOR MY SECOND SUICIDE ATTEMPT...
Interstellar is a feature film Sci-fi Drama by writer-director Christopher Nolan.

TRAUMA DICTIONARY

This poem is written as a Hermit Crab poem that utilizes a Dictionary definition template to define/expand on the term "Phantom Jam," which is the term for the domino effect of dense traffic crawling to a halt due to people unnecessarily braking.

DROWNING AS A MAGIC TRICK

This poem borrows its explanation of the three acts of magic from "The Prestige," a feature Drama by writer-director Christopher Nolan in which the three acts of a magic trick are narrated.

KICK / PUSH - AN ERASURE FOR THE MISCARRIAGE

This poem is an erasure of the song "Kick Push" by Chicago artist Lupe Fiasco from his debut album, *Food and Liquor.*

YOU GON' LEARN TODAY (ABOUT THIS LOVE)

This poem borrows the line "one nation under a groove" which is the name of the 1978 music album by the band Parliament Funkadelic.

IMMIGRATION AND CUSTOMS ENTOMOPHOBIA

This poem is written as a duplex, which is a form invented by the poet Jericho Brown. The title also is a play on I.C.E. which is the acronym for the US Agency of Immigration and Customs Enforcement. The "Toxic beauty" is the name of the Rainbow Milkweed Locust, which is a brightly colored, toxic grasshopper native to Madagascar and parts of Africa, known for feeding on milkweed and warning predators with its vivid colors.

UNICORN

This poem borrows its title from the term "Unicorn" which in sexual and relationship contexts, a unicorn is someone who joins a pre-existing couple, usually for sexual encounters, but sometimes for emotional or romantic involvement as well. The term comes from the rarity of finding someone willing to participate in this dynamic, much like the mythical creature.

THE ROPE REMEMBERS THE CRIMSON RECORD

This poem is written after the news of Trey Reed, A Delta State University student in Mississippi who was found dead by hanging on his campus. His death was ruled a suicide by the county coroner.

The poem borrows its title from the Crimson Record, which is a 2026 civil rights report documenting over 70 modern-day lynchings in the U.S. South, highlighting systemic racial violence and cover-ups released by the civil rights organization JULIAN since 2000, documenting more than 70 cases and over 150 fatal hate crimes targeting Black, Brown, immigrant, Indigenous, and LGBTQ+ communities. It serves as a contemporary follow-up to Ida B. Wells' 1895 A Red Record, which historically cataloged lynchings in the United States.

AT MY BROTHER'S WEDDING...
The poem includes the remixed line "Bitch Haha is you mad? Cuz my Pussy Pops severely and yours don't?" from a Vine video created by Vuser *dUhGreatOne*. The quote has since been remixed numerous times. The original video from which the quote is taken from was posted to Vine on April 21, 2014. The full line is as follows: "Bitch (laughs), why you mad? Cuz my pussy pops severely, and yours don't, huh?" Within a year of its posting, the video gained over 15 million loops, over 293 thousand likes, and over 208 thousand revines.

TRANSMOGRIFICATION SPELL...
This poem borrows a lyric from Chuck Brown's "it don't mean a thing."

AFTER ANOTHER CONVERSATION WITH MY MOTHER...
Is inspired by and borrows a line from Episode 24 in Season Four of the TV Half-Hour 90's Comedy, "The Fresh Prince of Bel Air" which aired on May 9, 1994. The episode is titled "Papa's Got a Brand New Excuse."

TONGES AS CASTING NETS...
In this poem, tchaseu si ne zeuzo zou is written in Bamileke. The poem is written in 16 couplets to reflect the 16 life cycles of shrimp from egg all the way to adult.

THE PH BALANCE OF PARENTING YOURSELF

The ph scale is a logarithmic scale used to measure the acidity or basicity of a solution. The scale reflects the concentration of hydrogen ions (H^+) in the solution, with lower pH values corresponding to higher acidity. It ranges from 0 to 14:

- A pH of 7 is considered neutral (like pure water).
- A pH less than 7 indicates an acidic solution.
- A pH greater than 7 indicates a basic (alkaline) solution

12 DISCIPLES...

This poem is after "everywhere in the world they hurt little black girls" by tafisha a. Edwards.

YA'ARBURNEE

This poem borrows its title from an Arabic word which does not exist in the English language. It means: the hopeful declaration that you will die before someone you love deeply, because you cannot stand to live without them. Literally, "may you bury me." The poem is also written as a Golden Shovel, which is a form invented by award-winning poet Terrance Hayes - utilizing the lyric *"Why is the world ugly when you made it in your image"* from the song "Dear God" by the Legendary Roots Crew from Philadelphia.

MARITIME IN LOUM

In this poem, there is a reference to Loum, a village in the Littoral region of Cameroun about a few hours north of the economic capital city of Douala.

WE PLAYED SADE AND WHITNEY...

The poem borrows the line "plastic off the sofa" from a song of the same name by Beyonce which first appeared on her RENAISSANCE album. "Bikutsi" in the poem is a traditional Cameroon dance.

STOCKHOLMED CHILD UNLEARNING

Is the third in a series using a black-out erasure form made with the i-765 Employment authorization form from the USCIS website.

I GOT FAMOUS FROM MY POEM ABOUT BEING RAPED…

This poem is a response to a poem written and performed by the Author titled "Piñatas" which was first published by Button Poetry in 2014 from the 2013 National Poetry Slam in Oakland and was one of the publication house's earlier viral poems.

MY SECOND TIME SKYDIVING…

In this poem, "Marimar" is a reference to the 1994 Mexican telenovela of the same name which was broadcasted by Canal de Las Estrellas. Additionally, "Ndol'e" is a traditional Cameroonian dish.

LAZARUS

This poem borrows its name from the man in the Bible who was resurrected by Jesus.

TATA CAROL…

different names for plantains exist in this poem. They are all the author's favorite.

MARIO KART UNMAKES…

"Mario Kart" is a racing video game that is a spin-off from the SUPER MARIO franchise by Nintendo.

ELEGY FOR THE BLUE SHELL

In this poem, the blue shell is another reference from the Mario Kart video game. It is a power-up item that, when launched, critically damages whoever is in first place at time of launch and potentially anyone in the proximity of the damage's blast radius.

OTHER POETIC TERMS THAT MAY BE FOUND IN THIS COLLECTION:

Anaphora
Often used in political speeches and occasionally in prose and poetry, anaphora is the repetition of a word or words at the beginning of successive phrases, clauses, or lines to create a sonic effect.

Found Poem
A prose text or texts reshaped by a poet into quasi-metrical lines.

Duplex
The duplex is a poetic form invented by poet Jericho Brown that subverts or is a "mash-up" of older poetic forms, such as the pantoum, the sonnet, and the ghazal. Brown first used this form in his third collection, *The Tradition* (Copper Canyon Press, 2019), which won the Pulitzer Prize for Poetry.

Ghazal
(Pronounciation: "guzzle") Originally an Arabic verse form dealing with loss and romantic love, medieval Persian poets embraced the ghazal, eventually making it their own. Consisting of syntactically and grammatically complete couplets, the form also has an intricate rhyme scheme.

Cleave
A cleave is a poetic form in which a poem is experienced three ways: poem 1 & 2 are two columns of text read separately down, poem 3 is the text of both columns read across to create the final poem.

Pantoum
A Malaysian verse form in quatrains with an intricate repeating pattern.

Erasure
Erasure poetry, the most common form of which is also called blackout poetry, is a poetic form in which a poet blacks out or in some way erases words from a preexisting source to create new poems.

Golden Shovel

Created by poet Terrance Hayes, this poetic form was designed to allow poets to pay tribute to existing work by poets they admire. A golden shovel borrows a line from an existing poem and uses each word from that line as the last word of each line in a new poem.

Ars Poetica

A poem that reflects on the art of poetry itself, discussing its purpose, methods, and nature.

Pregunta

The pregunta (Spanish for "question") is a traditional poetic form that pairs a question with an answer while mirroring the same meter and rhyme scheme. Its origin is in Spain, around the 14th century, used by court poets as a collaborative poetic game.

Apostrophe

An address to a dead or absent person, or personification as if he or she were present.

Hermit Crab

A Hermit Crab is a form popularized by FRONTIER POETRY Magazine & Publications as a yearly prompt. The form invites poets to take an existing form—like a recipe, glossary, index, test, or table of contents—and transform it into a poem. The goal is to make the borrowed structure poetically charged, impactful, and evocative, while still conveying substance, emotion, and truth.

Persona Poem

A persona poem is a type of poetry in which the poet writes from the perspective of a "persona," a character or voice distinct from their own. This can include historical figures, mythical beings, animals, inanimate objects, or entirely invented characters. The term "persona" comes from Latin, originally referring to a theatrical mask, highlighting the poem's use of artifice to explore different perspectives.

ABOUT THE AUTHOR

PAGES Matam (They/He), is a genderqueer med school drop-out turned award-winning multi-hyphenate, pleasure advocate and agent of imagination who was late to their own birth after nearly 11 months and now strives to write timely and timeless stories about those who defy the odds. Born and raised in Cameroun, Central Africa then blossomed in the DMV (Piscataway Land), they love Mario Kart, anime, and fried plantains as much as crafting High-concept character-driven TV dramas, experimental shorts, and vulnerable poetry at the intersection of immigrant, Black, and Queer narratives. Fluent in 4 languages, their work as a film-poet is fueled by Toni Morrison's words: "the function of freedom is to free someone else," challenging systems of power to move towards inclusive and ethical liberation. PAGES is a National Poetry Slam Champion and touring Burlesque performer as seen on BET, TV One, Essence Festival, MACY's, The Kennedy Center, Apollo Theater, & TEDx. Additionally, they were named a Google x The Guardian Rising Voices, Cultural Ambassador to the National Fair Housing Alliance, a 2024 John Singleton X PAFF Short Films Finalist, and an inaugural creative with Keke Palmer's KeyTV. Additionally, they've earned multiple poetry and screenwriting fellowships including Callaloo @ Brown University, GLAAD Black Queer Creatives, DEFINE AMERICAN, Artist Disruptors by the Center for Cultural Power, Circle of Confusion Writers Discovery, and TRIBE at SuperSpecial by Amy Aniobi.

BOOK RECOMMENDATIONS FROM THE AUTHOR

WASH by Ebony Stewart

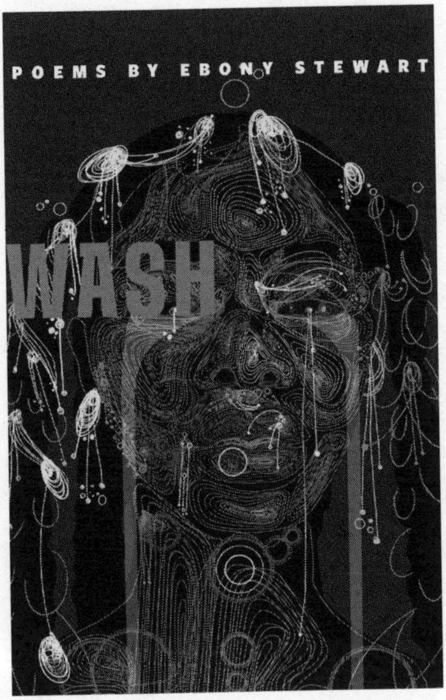

In this latest and even more spectacular offering from Ebony Stewart, we wade through a deep examination of grief and unbecoming. *WASH* is both how we drown and how we come up for air. A praise dance and a cleansing, that has us begging to open the floodgates of our small victories to wash over all of our sufferings.

Born in a Second Language by Akosua Zimba Afiriyie-Hwedie

Born in a Second Language is a sharp machete cutting through the heart. It is a riot and a balm forcing one to examine all of the uncomfortable and gut-wrenching griefs at the intersection of identity, gender & sexuality, womanhood, and culture. A poetic ethnography that is profound as it rebellious. A more than worthwhile journey interconnected by language and the longings it often creates.

Cottonmouth by Miya Coleman

Cottonmouth is Chicago Black girl alchemy, deconstructing and reconstructing all of our notions of love, family, growth and the way shame wounds us. Offering a reckoning in every stanza, Miya Coleman takes us through a wild ride of the personal and the political that will leave you never wanting to get off.

OTHER BOOKS BY BUTTON POETRY

If you enjoyed this book, please consider checking out some of our others, below. Readers like you allow us to keep broadcasting and publishing. Thank you!

Francis Dylan Waguespack, *Tooth Gaps in the Archives*
Gigi Bella, *without the frills*
Buddy Wakefield, *Stunt Water*
Ollie Schminkey, *Don't be Afraid to be Bad*
Carson Wolfe, *Coin Laundry at Midnight*
Adrienne Novy, *good luck in the real world*
Rachel Camacho, *Pink Elephant*
Aly Acevedo, *My Dear Cult Leader*
Kristina Percy, *Both True*
FreeQuency, *(On |Un-)Becoming*
Hailey Tran, *an everyday occurrence*
Mickie Kennedy, *Glandscapes*
Chelsea Guevara, *Cipota*
Daniel Elias Galicia, *Still Desert*
Jared Singer, *Forgotten Necessities*
Meg Ford, *Wild/Hurt*
Jalen Eutsey, *Bubble Gum Stadium*
Najya Williams, *on a date with disappointment*
L.E. Bowman, *Shapeshifter*
Ebony Stewart, *WASH*
Phil SaintDenisSanchez, *before & after our bodies*
Josh Tvrdy, *Smut Psalm*
Neil Hilborn, *About Time*
Eric Sirota, *The Rent Eats First*
Zach Goldberg, *I'd Rather Be Destroyed*
Topaz Winters, *Portrait of my Body as a Crime I'm Still Committing*
Zach Goldberg, *I'd Rather Be Destroyed*
Matt Coonan, *Toy Gun*

Available at buttonpoetry.com/shop and more!

BUTTON POETRY BEST SELLERS